Play the Game

Basketball

D1395688

Play the Game

Basketball

David Titmuss

WARD LOCK

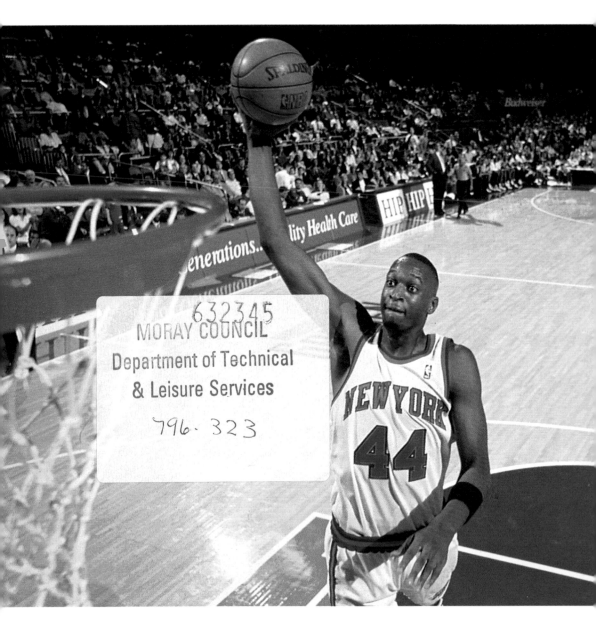

Half-title page: *Charles Barkley prepares to shoot for the basket*

Title page: *Allen Iverson of Philadelphia demonstrating use of his left hand while going around Tyus Edney of Sacramento*

Above: *John Wallace of the New York Knicks dunking during a match against Houston*

Contents

Foreword   6

History & development of basketball   8

Equipment & terminology   16

The game – a guide   30

Rules clinic   42

Technique   52

Useful addresses   78

Rules clinic index   79

General index   80

Foreword

Basketball is probably the fastest-growing team sport in the world, especially among young people, yet players of any age can get enormous enjoyment from this quick and exciting sport. This book will ensure you get the most out of playing or watching the game.

On behalf of the English Basketball Association I am delighted to endorse and highly recommend this excellent book to all aspiring basketballers. The crisp text and clear illustrations ensure that its meaning is readily accessible to the novice and an ideal refresher for the more experienced performer.

The history of the sport is well documented and makes fascinating reading. Basketball equipment is thoroughly covered so that, when you first walk on to a court, you will be familiar with the surroundings. There are some peculiar terms unique to basketball, and these are covered in an interesting terminology section. The rules of basketball are covered in a simple Game Guide but for those of you who want to delve into the finer points and intricacies which all rules have, then no stone is unturned in the cleverly designed Rules Clinic. The remainder of the book is devoted to basketball technique.

I can think of no one more suitable to write about the sport of basketball than the author, David Titmuss, who is one of the country's most knowledgeable, talented and committed coaches. His work with the English Senior Men's team, which under his leadership enjoyed a period of unprecedented success, firmly established his international reputation. Coach Titmuss holds the English Basketball Association's National Coach Award, is a frequent lecturer at advanced coach training courses and has considerable practical experience coaching in the USA, with the England team, and throughout Europe.

Brian E. Coleman
Former Technical Officer
English Basketball Association

History & development of **basketball**

Unlike many sports, basketball can pinpoint its exact origins to one day in 1891 when Canadian-born Dr James Naismith invented a brand-new game, as opposed to evolving it from another sport.

Naismith was a leader of the International YMCA Training School at Springfield, Massachussetts and was set the task of devising a new game for his students who were fed up with conventional forms of gymnastics. And so he set about inventing his new game which, because the basic principal was to secure possession of the ball and throw it into the opponents' basket, he called basketball.

Although Naismith's game was brand new, evidence suggests that he got his idea from other, older sports.

A form of basketball was played in ancient Central and South American civilizations. Playing courts bounded by stone walls and set among trees have been found on the Yucatán Peninsula of South America dating to the seventh century BC. The game, known as *pok-tapok*, took place as part of a religious festival. It was played with a ball filled with sacred plants and the ball had to be hit into an elevated 'goal' using only the knees, thighs and hips. The goals consisted of a flat slab with a hole in the middle and it was through this hole that the ball had to pass . . . a bit like scoring a basket in basketball.

In Mexico, in the sixteenth century, the game of *Ollamalitzli* was similar, but played with a solid rubber ball being thrown through a stone ring. Rumour has it that the player who successfully threw the ball into the ring could claim the clothes of all spectators . . . a bit like strip basketball!

A seventeenth-century engraving depicts a game similar to basketball and the *Encyclopedia of Athletics* (1818) lists a game played in Florida in which players threw a ball into a basket attached to the top of a pole.

Despite these precedents, though, there is no denying that credit for the playing of basketball as we know it today goes to Dr James Naismith.

Naismith wanted a game which prevented physical contact and consequently running with the ball was outlawed in his first set of rules. Naismith also saw his game demanding skill and not physical strength. That is still the case today, although it does help to be strong and above average height.

Simplicity was uppermost in Naismith's mind when he drew up his first set of rules in December 1891. A look at his first rules will bear this out, and closer examination of his rules, and cross reference with the game guide on pages 30–40 will show that many of his original thirteen rules form the basis of the present-day game.

BASKETBALL'S FIRST RULES

1. The ball, an ordinary Association football, may be thrown in any direction with one or both hands.
2. The ball may be batted in any direction with one or both hands, but never with the fist.
3. A player cannot run with the ball. The player must throw it from the spot on which he catches it. Allowance to be made for the man who catches the ball while running at a good speed.

4. The ball must be held in or between the hands. The arms or the body must not be used for holding it.

5. No shouldering, holding, pushing, striking or tripping in any way the person of an opponent shall be allowed. The first infringement of this rule by any person shall count as a foul; the second shall disqualify him until the next goal is made or, if there was evident intent to injure the person, for the whole of the game. No substitution shall be allowed.

6. A foul is striking at the ball with the fist, violations of rules three and four, and such as described in rule five.

7. If either side makes three consecutive fouls it shall count as a goal for the opponents (consecutive means without the opponents in the meantime making a foul).

8. A goal shall be made when the ball is thrown or batted from the ground into the basket and stays there, providing those defending the goal do not touch or disturb the goal. If the ball rests on the edge and the opponents move the basket it shall count as a goal.

9. When the ball goes out of bounds it shall be thrown into the field and played by the first person touching it. In case of dispute the umpire shall throw it straight into the field, the thrower-in is allowed five seconds. If he holds it longer it shall go to the opponents. If any side persists in delaying the game, the umpire shall call a foul on them.

10. The umpire shall be the judge of the men and shall note the fouls and notify the referee when three consecutive fouls have been made. He shall have the power to disqualify men according to rule five.

11. The referee shall be the judge of the ball and decide when it is in play in bounds, to which side it belongs, and shall keep the time. He shall decide when a goal has been made and keep account of the goals with any other duties that are usually performed by a referee.

12. The time shall be two fifteen-minute halves with five minutes' rest between.

13. The side making the most goals in that time shall be declared the winners.

It was to these rules of 20 January 1892 that the first game of basketball took place at the Springfield YMCA gymnasium. Two peach baskets nailed to a balcony 3m (10ft) from the ground were installed and these formed the goals. Being out of reach from the players it was another example of the new game demanding the best of skills from the player who was required to throw the ball accurately into the 'goal'.

Surprisingly Naismith's rules did not stipulate how many players were to be on each side. He suggested any number between three and forty could play. But that first game at Springfield consisted of nine students per team and this was felt to be an ideal number at first.

Basketball proved to be so popular that other colleges and organizations requested copies of Naismith's rules.

Basketball had arrived and its early success lay in its simplicity and the fact that it could be played on any area, large or small. The year after its debut at Springfield the first game of basketball was played in England when it was introduced by Mme Bergman-Osterberg at Hampstead Physical Training College.

By 1895 players had become so skilled it was agreed that the number in a team should be restricted to either five, seven or nine, depending upon the size of the playing area available. But it was not long before this was standardized at today's figure of five.

Also, in 1895, the YMCA obtained a copy of the rules and modified them slightly for their women members to provide a less strenuous game, thus bringing about the birth of netball.

Naismith had developed one of the most popular participant sports but he overlooked one important detail: how to retrieve the ball every time a 'goal' was scored. Initially a ladder was used to get the ball out of the basket. But, as players got better, and goals were scored more frequently, a lot of time was wasted with retrieving the ball. Towards the end of the century, however, the basket was replaced by a metal ring which had a bottomless net attached to it. And so the basketball ball retriever was made redundant. Oh well, that's life!

Right from the start, basketball competitions were organized through the YMCA movement, and in 1901 the first collegiate league was inaugurated. Basketball made its debut as a demonstration sport at the 1904 St Louis Olympics but all teams were from the United States. However, when it was included as an exhibition sport at the Paris Olympics of 1924, teams from France, Italy, United

States and Great Britain competed. The London Central YMCA won the gold medal. Despite efforts, largely those of Dr Forest Allen, to get basketball included at the 1928, and then 1932, Olympics as either a full or demonstration sport, it was neglected on both occasions.

However, the sport gained credibility in 1932 when the international ruling body, the International Amateur Basketball Federation (Federation Internationale de Basketball Amateur – FIBA) was formed. Seven countries attended a meeting at Geneva and Renato William Jones (Italian-born son of an Englishman) was appointed the first secretary-general. Today there are more than 200 member nations of FIBA.

Allen and Jones were successful in their attempts to get basketball included in the XIth Olympics at Berlin in 1936. Twenty-two nations competed in the first full Olympic tournament which, unusually, was played outdoors. The United States were the first champions and one of the referees was Avery Brundage, later to become the President of the International Olympic Committee. The medals were presented by the game's inventor, Dr Naismith, who died three years later at the age of 78.

The game soon spread worldwide after gaining Olympic status, thanks largely to the efforts of the YMCA movement and American servicemen who introduced the sport at each of their 'ports-of-call'.

Minor adjustments were made to Naismith's rules over the years. Dribbling became legal; a backboard was added behind the basket, thus making rebounding an important part of the game, and the ball became unique in size and weight, as opposed to using a standard Association football.

Two other significant rule changes were introduced. The first in the 1920s saw the introduction of the rule that the player fouled had to take free shots himself. Previously, a specialist 'free-shooter' was employed. And in 1936 the jump-ball, which was used at the centre circle after every score, was abolished. Consequently, the game was speeded up and became more strenuous.

Specific timing regulations, time-outs and increase in size of the restricted area under the basket have all been important changes and additions which have helped to make basketball one of the best spectator sports.

In America, spectators have ample opportunity to watch basketball at the highest level, and indeed basketball is one of the most successful televised sports. The NCAA (Collegiate game) has organized its championship since 1938 and the National Basketball Association (NBA) gained Major League status in 1949, although the professional game was born in the United States at the turn of the twentieth century. The NBA offers all that is best in the professional game while the entertaining Harlem Globetrotters team provides circus-like performances.

Known the world over as 'the trotters', they were formed in 1927 by Abraham Saperstein, who took his team of all-black players around the United States giving exhibitions and demonstrations. They gradually introduced skilful and entertaining routines into their play, which eventually developed into a comedy routine with such well-known exponents as Meadowlark Lemon. They adopted the music of 'Sweet Georgia Brown' as their theme tune, and it has been heard in most countries worldwide as the Globetrotters have taken their own brand of entertainment to all corners of the globe.

In Great Britain the English Basketball Association was founded in 1936 and Holylake YMCA were the first winners of the National Championship. The YMCA movement has played a crucial role in basketball's development in Britain as well as in the United States. The Scottish, Irish and Welsh Associations were formed as independent Associations in 1947, 1946 and 1956 respectively.

The sport dropped in popularity in Britain in the early 1960s. But a dramatic growth period got under way in the 1970s when the English Basketball Association appointed its first full-time administrator, Mel Welch.

Club sponsorship came into the British game in a big way in 1973, and in 1975 attendances broke the 100,000 barrier. Famous names have been brought into basketball, and the Manchester United, Bolton Wanderers and Glasgow Rangers football teams have acquired franchises over the years. The end-of-season play-offs are the highlight of the season in Britain with the final rounds being played at Wembley Arena.

Women also play basketball – and not only netball, as many people believe. The women's game was included in the Olympic programme for the first time in 1976. They have also had their own World Championships since 1953, coming just three years after

Argentina won the inaugural men's World Championship.

In 1989 FIBA eliminated the distinction between amateur and professional players, a move that, three years later, saw a team of NBA stars such as Michael Jordan, Magic Johnson and Larry Bird taking part in (and winning) the Olympic Games in Barcelona.

Although the NBA remains the premier club basketball league in the world, it is no longer solely the preserve of American players. In recent years players from Europe, Australia and Africa have been signed up by the American pro league. The same is true of the new Women's NBA, which had its inaugural season in summer 1997.

We would like to re-emphasize that basketball is now played by both men and women, and boys and girls. But for simplicity all references in this book are made to he and him. Please don't treat this as any form of chauvinism . . . it's just that it makes the text clearer and simpler to read.

Basketball is growing in popularity all the time, both as a participant and spectator sport. As a participant sport there is no restriction on the aspirant player. Certainly, most basketball players are tall, but don't let that put you off because there is always a place for the skilful player, irrespective of size. As a spectator sport, basketball offers all the excitement that other team sports such as soccer can provide but with three additional important factors. Firstly, being played on a smaller area, all the action can be seen at close range . . . and indoors. Secondly, there is always a result; there are no draws in basketball except in ties played over two legs, where no overtime would be played if the scores are level in either leg. Thirdly, basketball matches are places of family entertainment. Men, women and children can attend a basketball match and mix with supporters of opposing sides and the air of friendliness is maintained. A sport offering that these days can only be a good one to get involved with.

Play the Game: Basketball will give you an insight into the game – whether it be as an aspiring youngster wishing to take the game up, or as the spectator who wants to enjoy the thrills and excitement of basketball from a cosy position either in the stands or in your armchair. Either way, *Basketball* will improve your knowledge of the game.

US Olympic player Dawn Staley working the ball quickly up the court in a confident, fluent movement

Equipment & terminology

As with all sports, a thorough background knowledge of the playing area and equipment you will encounter is especially useful whether you are playing or watching the game of basketball.

Before we introduce you to the rules of basketball, you ought to familiarize yourself with the playing area, playing equipment and some of the terminology you will encounter when playing or watching the game. Let's start with the court.

The court

Basketball can be played indoors or outdoors. But at senior and international level it is exclusively an indoor game.

The playing area, known as the court, is rectangular and should be a level, hard surface and free from any obstructions which may be dangerous to the players. Ideally the playing surface should be wood or any suitable artificial surface that will provide the ball with a good and consistent bounce.

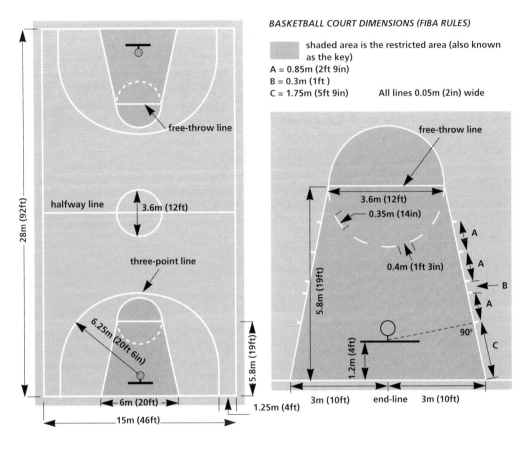

BASKETBALL COURT DIMENSIONS (FIBA RULES)

shaded area is the restricted area (also known as the key)

A = 0.85m (2ft 9in)
B = 0.3m (1ft)
C = 1.75m (5ft 9in)   All lines 0.05m (2in) wide

free-throw line

28m (92ft)

halfway line   3.6m (12ft)

three-point line

6.25m (20ft 6in)

6m (20ft)
15m (46ft)
1.25m (4ft)
5.8m (19ft)

free-throw line

3.6m (12ft)
0.35m (14in)

A
A
B
A

0.4m (1ft 3in)

90°
C

5.8m (19ft)

1.2m (4ft)

3m (10ft)   end-line   3m (10ft)

The court measures 28m (92ft) in length and 15m (46ft) in width. Variations of 2m (6ft 6in) on length and 1m (3ft 3in) on width are permitted but any variations must be proportional to each other.

A clearance of 7m (24ft) between the floor and ceiling should exist and the court should be adequately lit and no unsightly shadows cast. The lighting should not be so positioned that it will hinder the vision and sight of any of the players or officials.

The court should be bounded by boundary lines at least 2m (6ft 6in) from any obstructions including seating, scorers'/time-keepers' tables, etc. The lines that extend along the length of the court are known as the side-lines and those across the width are the end-lines. All boundary lines should be clearly marked and be 5cm (2in) wide.

One of the three restraining circles, with a radius of 1.8m (6ft), is drawn at the centre of the court. The court is divided into two equal halves by the halfway line, which provides each team with a front court and a back court. A team's front court is that part of the court between the opponents' end-line and the nearer edge of the halfway line. Their back court is the other half of the court including the halfway line. The front and back courts are important as you will find out later when we discuss the rules in detail in The Game – A Guide on pages 30–41.

The free-throw line is basketball's equivalent to the penalty spot in soccer. It is a line 3.6m (12ft) long drawn parallel to the end-line and is 5.8m (19ft) from the inner edge of the end-line to the

BASKETBALL COURT DIMENSIONS (NBA RULES)

shaded area is the restricted area (also known as the key)
A = 0.9m (3ft)
B = 0.3m (1ft)
C = 1.2m (4ft)   All lines 0.05m (2in) wide

1.8m (6ft) radius outside

free-throw line

35cm (14in)

3.65m (12ft)

1.8m (6ft)

4.8m (16ft)

end-line

A

A

B

A

C

Optimum length 28.6m (94ft)

Optimum width 15.24m (50ft) inside side-lines

C
A
B
A
A

7.24m (23ft 9in)

6.4m (21ft)

A

1.8m (6ft) radius outside

halfway line

0.6m (2ft) radius inside

three-point line

5.8m (19ft)

8.53m (28ft)

A

4.8m (16ft)

further edge of the free-throw line. The centre of the free-throw line should be in line with the centre point of the end-line.

At each end of the court is a restricted area; again its importance will become clear in The Game – A Guide chapter. Under FIBA rules the restricted area is bounded by lines drawn from each end of the free-throw line to a point 3m (10ft) either side of the centre of the end-line. The restricted area is further extended by a semi-circle drawn from the centre of the free-throw line and with a radius of 1.8m (6ft). The semi-circle extends into the restricted area to make a complete circle, but that part of the circle in the restricted area is shown only by a broken line. These two restraining circles at the free-throw lines and the one at the halfway line form the three restraining circles at which a jump-ball can be used to re-start the game.

During free throws players must stand at spaces marked along the restricted area. The first of these spaces is marked 1.75m (5ft 9in) (NBA: 2.1m/7ft) from the inside edge of the end-line. The others are as shown on the diagrams opposite (for NBA competition) and on page 17 (FIBA).

Because basketball has a three-point basket (see page 26) the area from where such a score can be made is defined by the drawing of an arc with a radius of 6.25m (20ft 6in) in FIBA competition and 7.24m (23ft 9in) in NBA competition from the centre of the basket. It forms a semi-circle with each end terminating at the end-line. In the NBA the edges of the arc closest to the side-lines are drawn parallel to the side-lines to allow the shooter space to stand.

The backboard and basket

The backboard is 1.2m (4ft) from the end-line and measures 1.8m (6ft) by 1.05m (3ft 5in). It should be made of hard wood 3cm (1in) thick or of a suitable transparent material but with a similar rigidity to wood. The front surface must be flat and white (unless it is transparent). A rectangle measuring 59cm (2ft) by 45cm (1ft 6in) should be drawn on the backboard. The bottom line of the rectangle should be level with the top of the net. The lines of this rectangle should be 5cm (2in) wide. A 5cm (2in) border should be drawn along the outside perimeter of the backboard and in a colour contrasting with the background.

The backboard should be positioned above the court and with

THE BACKBOARD AND BASKET
Note the rectangular 'marker' directly above the basket

All lines 0.05m (2in) wide

The basket and support

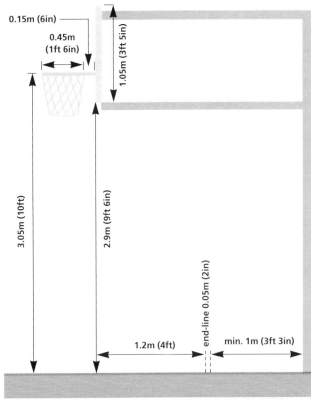

its lower edge 2.9m (9ft 6in) above the floor. The backboard should be positioned at a central point between the two side-lines and the supports should be at least 1m (3ft 3in) outside the end-line painted in a colour contrasting with the background so players can easily see the backboard. In the interests of safety it should also be covered in a padded protective material.

Attached to each backboard is the all-important basket. The ring, which supports the net (or basket), is made of solid iron, has an inside diameter of 45cm (1ft 6in) and should be painted orange. The ring should be rigidly attached to the backboard and at a point 3.05m (10ft) above the floor. The net, which is attached to the ring, is made of cord and is 40cm (15in) long. It should be wide enough for the ball to freely pass through.

The ball

The ball is round and the outer casing should be leather, rubber or other suitable synthetic material. Its circumference should be 75–78cm (29½–30¼in) and its weight 567–650g (20–22oz). It should be inflated to a pressure so that when it is dropped from a height of 1.8m (6ft) (measured from the floor to the bottom of the ball) on to the playing surface, it will rebound to a height of 1.2–1.4m (4ft–4ft 7in) (measured to the top of the ball).

THE BALL
Circumference 75–78cm (29½–30¼in)
Weight 567–650gm (20–22oz)

In addition to that equipment already mentioned, the home team is normally responsible for providing the following: a clock, time-out watch, device for displaying to players and spectators how much time is left on the thirty-seconds/twenty-four-seconds rule (see The Game – A Guide), an official score sheet, scoreboard visible to spectators and players, markers displaying the numbers 1 to 5 for use by the scorer to indicate how many fouls a player commits, and two team-foul markers, which are red and placed on the scorer's table to indicate a seventh-player foul by a team.

Clothing

Each player in a team should wear the same outfit, which must not clash with that of the opposing team. Each player should wear a numbered shirt and no two players in the same team should wear the same number. FIBA shirts are numbered 4 to 15 while NBA permits other combinations – their criteria being whether the number can be easily understood when signalled by a referee.

Loose-fitting shorts (for mobility) and sleeveless vests are the standard attire. Many players like to wear a T-shirt under their vest for added comfort and this should be of a similar colour to the vest. Players who wear long undershorts are also required by most leagues to match the colour of the undershorts to the shorts they are wearing.

CLOTHING

Basketball shoes should be rubber-soled and with protected ankle supports, although these are not necessary. Generally players in a team should wear shoes of the same basic colour (usually black or white). Most important of all, make sure your clothing is comfortable. It is important to wear towelled socks; and it is not a bad idea to buy a pair of shoes a little too big to enable you to wear two pairs of socks, which will reduce the risk of blistering.

Right, that's basketball equipment. Now for some terms you will encounter.

TERMINOLOGY

Assist A pass that allows the receiver an easy, close score.

Back court The half of the court containing a team's basket.

Note the rubber soles for good traction

Back court violation When the team in possession passes the ball back into their own half of the court.

Basket The basket is basketball's goal. It is also the term used to denote a successful score. A successful basket is worth one, two or three points.

Centre Sometimes the key player in a team. He is usually, but not always, the tallest player and should be capable of scoring from close range and from rebounds. He is also known as the pivot.

Charged time-out FIBA coaches may request two time-outs per half, each one lasting up to one minute during which time they can instruct their players. If a game goes into overtime, then one time-out is allowed per extra period played. The NBA allows seven time-outs per game plus a twenty-second time-out; there is also a

David Robinson of San Antonio Spurs shows his prowess at the dunk – the basket is 3.05m (10ft) off the ground

maximum of three time-outs per overtime period. It also entitles players and coaches to call time-outs – unlike FIBA.

Disqualifying foul Any blatant disregard for the rules and unsportsmanlike conduct will result in a player being removed from the game permanently.

Double foul When two players from opposing sides commit personal fouls against each other. Play is re-started with a jump-ball.

Double team Term used when two defenders mark one attacker.

Dunk When a basket is scored by a player jumping with the ball above the net and thrusting it down through the net. Also known as a 'stuff'.

Fake A dummy with the body and/or ball in order to wrong-foot your opponent.

Fast break A quick move out of defence after gaining possession of the ball and designed to take the opposing team by surprise before they have a chance to re-form their defence.

The free throw

Field goal A scoring shot from open play. It is worth two or three points.

Five-second rule A closely guarded player in possession of the ball must pass, shoot or dribble the ball within five seconds of gaining possession.

Flagrant foul see Unsportsmanlike foul.

Forwards Tall players who take up a position in the front court, normally between the side-lines and restricted area.

Free throw A free throw at the basket without any interference from the opposing team. The throw is taken from the free-throw line and each successful throw is worth one point. Free throws are awarded for fouls – technical or personal.

Front court The half of the court in which your opponent's basket is situated, and the half of the court your team attacks.

Full court press A defensive tactic employing the entire court not just the back court.

Guards Usually smaller than the forwards, the guards are good dribblers and passers. They should be excellent ball-handlers, and also be able to shoot accurately from long distance. The guard is the playmaker of the side.

Held ball When two or more players of opposing teams have one or both hands firmly on the ball at the same time. Play re-starts with a jump-ball.

Javelin pass A single-handed, overhead pass in which the ball is thrown in a motion similar to the throw of a baseball.

Jump-ball A method of starting and re-starting play. The ball is thrown up by an official between two opposing players who have to attempt to gain possession for their team.

THE JAVELIN PASS
Use it to throw long distances

Key The restricted area. It is called the key because it resembles a keyhole. The semi-circle forms part of the key.

Man-to-man marking A form of defence whereby a defensive player marks a specific attacking player rather than defending an opponent only when he moves into a particular area of court.

Outlet pass The first pass of the defensive team after a rebound. Often it is a quick pass out to a player near to the side-line.

Out-of-bounds A player or the ball is out-of-bounds if he/it touches the floor on or outside the boundary lines.

Overtime Drawn games do not exist in basketball. So if the scores are level at the end of normal time, extra periods of overtime – each lasting five minutes – are played.

Personal foul A foul against an opponent whether the ball is in play, alive or dead. Blocking, holding, pushing, charging, tripping and impeding all constitute personal fouls.

OUT-OF-BOUNDS
A player is deemed to be out-of-bounds if part of his foot is on, or over, a side- or end-line

A PERSONAL FOUL
Deliberately trying to hinder your
opponent is a personal foul

Pivot see Centre.

Strong side The side of the court in which the attacking team has possession of the ball.

Stuff see Dunk.

Substitute Up to five substitutes per team are allowed.

Technical foul Can be committed by a player, coach, substitutes or team followers. Anything that is against the spirit of the game can be basically described as a technical foul.

Ten-seconds rule Within ten seconds of getting the ball a team must advance the ball over the halfway line.

Three-point basket A basket scored from open play outside the three-point arc.

Three-point play When a player is fouled in the process of scoring a two-point basket and gains another point from the free throw.

Three-seconds rule No player may stand in that part of the opposing restricted area between the end-line and free-throw line for more than three seconds when his own team has possession of the ball.

Time-out A time-out can be called by a coach when the clock is stopped after an official signals:
a. A violation.
b. A foul.
c. A held ball.
d. An unusual delay in re-starting the game following a dead-ball.
e. Suspension of play following injury.
f. Suspension of play for any other reason.
g. When the thirty-seconds signal is sounded.
h. After a basket is scored against the team that has requested a charged time-out.

Unsportsmanlike foul A personal foul which, in the opinion of the official, was deliberate. In addition to the offending player having a personal foul charged against him, two free throws are awarded plus possession of the ball at the halfway line. The NBA refers to unsportsmanlike fouls as flagrant fouls.

Weak side The side of the court opposite where the attacking side has possession of the ball.

Zone defence In FIBA this is the marking of attacking players when they move into specific areas of the court as opposed to man-to-man marking. The NBA however has illegal defence rules in order to outlaw the use of the zone defence.

With the palms of his hands facing the ball and so ready to take possession, Alonzo Mourning of Miami uses his arms to attempt to block a shot by Scottie Pippen of Chicago

The game –
a guide

Basketball is a fast-moving, all-action game. The object is simple: to get the ball into the opposing net in order to score points.

To get into a scoring position however, the ball must be dribbled or passed around the court using only the hands. That is when it starts becoming a bit more difficult.

As we have already seen, a team consists of no more than ten players, with only five on court at any one time. However, in tournaments where a team has to play more than five games, then the number of players in each team may be increased to twelve.

One member of the team is appointed captain. If, for any reason, the captain leaves the court then he must inform the referee which team-mate will take over his role.

Officials
A game of basketball is controlled by a referee and umpire who are assisted by a timekeeper, scorer and a thirty-seconds operator (twenty-four-seconds operator in the NBA). The officials should wear basketball shoes, long black trousers and a grey shirt so as to be easily distinguishable from the players.

The referee and umpire jointly control the game and take up positions on opposite sides of the court so they can see all of the action (and infringements) between them. Before each jump-ball and after each foul they swap sides. The referee has ultimate control and he is the official who makes a decision on any point not specifically mentioned in the rules of the game.

The scorer also plays an important role. In addition to keeping a chronological check of points scored he must also record the personal and technical fouls called against each player. He also keeps a note of the time-outs charged to each team, notes the starting line-ups of each team and any subsequent changes in playing personnel by way of substitutions. He's certainly a busy person is the scorer.

The timekeeper maintains a record of playing time and time of stoppage(s) as provided within the rules. He is also responsible for timing the time-outs and for indicating the end of each half or overtime.

The final official is the thirty-seconds/twenty-four-seconds operator. He controls the thirty-second clock, which is started by him the moment a team takes possession of the ball.

Now that we have described the officials, let's now see how the actual game is played.

How basketball is played

The FIBA game is divided into two halves, each lasting twenty minutes and with an interval of (normally) ten minutes, while the NBA game periods comprise four quarters of twelve minutes each.

The game is started with a jump-ball in the centre circle. The visiting team has choice of baskets in the first half. Ends are changed after the interval. If the game is played at a neutral venue then a choice of baskets in the first half is decided by a toss of a coin. The jump-ball starts each subsequent half or extra period of play. It is performed by the referee throwing the ball up into the air between two opposing players who each stand in that half of the centre circle nearer to their own basket.

The ball cannot be touched until it has reached its greatest height. A player involved in the jump-ball may touch the ball twice only. He must not touch it again until one of the eight players not included in the jump-ball has touched it, or it has touched the floor,

OFFICIALS' SIGNALS

two points

three-point attempt

three points – successful shot

cancel score/cancel play

time-out

charged time-out

substitution

time in

travelling

illegal dribble

three-seconds rule – infraction

personal foul

personal foul. No free throws

free-throw penalty

to designate offender

pushing

illegal use of hands

holding

blocking

charging

foul by team in control of the ball

technical foul

unsportsmanlike/flagrant foul

disqualifying foul

double foul

jump-ball

ball returned to back court

three free throws

two free throws

one free throw

timed-out

re-setting of thirty-seconds/twenty-four-seconds clock

THE JUMP–BALL
The jump-ball is used to start the game

ring or backboard. All non-jumpers must stand outside the centre circle of the court.

Once a team has possession of the ball, the player with the ball may dribble it by bouncing it on the ground using one hand to do so. He may, alternatively, pass it to a team-mate. The eventual aim is to get the ball to a player in a suitable position to shoot at the net in the hope of successfully scoring points.

If the ball is successfully thrown through the net it is worth three points if thrown from outside the three-point line, otherwise it is worth two points. A goal from a free throw (which will be explained later) is worth one point. The winning team is the team scoring the most points, NOT the team obtaining the most baskets.

After a field goal has been scored, play is not re-started with another jump-ball. The ball is returned to play by a member of the non-scoring team who stands at a point out-of-bounds at the end of the court where the goal was made. Play is also re-started by this method after the last free throw, if successful. If the ball goes out of play over the side-lines it is returned by a member of the team who did not last play the ball by means of a throw-in.

International star and celebrity Michael Jordan in action – this time for the Chicago Bulls

Play resumes until the end of forty minutes (NBA: forty-eight minutes) playing time and the team with the most points is deemed the winner. However, if the scores are level at the end of normal playing time then an extra period of five minutes is played. As many extra periods as required to find a winner are played. There is no limit on the number of extra periods.

Timing regulations

To ensure basketball maintains its fluency and that the forty minutes (NBA: forty-eight minutes) is actually utilized as playing time, there are various timing regulations which are observed.

To indicate the start of a game the clock is activated the moment the ball reaches its highest point at the jump-ball and is touched by one of the jumpers. The game clock is stopped at the end of each half or extra period and when the official blows his whistle for any of the following:

a. A violation.

b. A foul.

c. A held ball.

d. Delay in re-starting the game following a dead-ball.

e. Suspension of play following injury.

f. Suspension of play for any reason as ordered by the officials.

g. When the thirty-second/twenty-four-second signal is sounded.

h. When a field goal is scored against the team whose coach has requested a time-out.

i. (NBA only) After every basket in the last minute of the first three quarters and after every basket in the last two minutes of the fourth quarter.

Charged time-outs are permitted by a team's coach. He is allowed to call a maximum of two per half and must indicate his request to the scorer who conveys the request to the officials. As soon as the ball becomes dead the clock is stopped and the charged time-out lasting one minute begins. It is important to realise, for timing purposes, when a ball is in play and when it is alive.

The ball is in play when:

a. The official enters the centre circle to carry out the jump-ball.

b. The official enters the free-throw area to effect a free throw.

c. The player at a side-line possession has taken up an out-of-bounds position and taken possession of the ball.

In the above instances the ball becomes alive when:

a. The ball, having reached its highest peak at the jump-ball, is touched by a player involved in the jump-ball.

b. The official gives the ball to a player entitled to take the free throw.

c. The ball touches a player in play from a side-line possession.

It is important that the following timings are fully understood:

The three-seconds rule A player must not remain for more than three seconds in that part of the opponent's restricted area between the end-line and farthest edge of the free-throw line, while his team is in control of the ball.

The five-seconds rule A closely guarded player who does not pass, shoot, roll or dribble the ball within five seconds shall be penalized and have a violation called against him. A player out-of-bounds must put the ball in play within five seconds or possession goes to the defensive team.

The ten-seconds rule When a team gains possession of a live ball in its own back court it must, within ten seconds, cause the ball to go into its front court. If it does not then a violation is called. If a team has possession in its front court, it must not cause the ball to go into its own back court.

The thirty-seconds rule Within thirty seconds of gaining control of a live ball a team must shoot at goal. Failure to do so is a violation. In the NBA the team must shoot within twenty-four seconds.

Any violations of these timing regulations are penalized with loss of ball to the opposing team.

Moving the ball around the court

It must be remembered that the ball can be played only with the hands. Touching the ball with the leg or foot is a violation, unless it is accidental. The ball must not be played with a clenched fist, nor must it be carried.

When dribbling, the ball must be bounced on to the floor and with only one hand. The dribble is deemed to have ended when a player touches the ball with both hands simultaneously, or when he allows the ball to come to rest in one or both hands. The player may not dribble again until after he has taken a shot or the

THE DRIBBLE
Dribbling is one way of moving the ball around the court – but passing is better

ball has been played by another person.

When a player gets possession of the ball from another player, or from a rebounded attempt at a basket, he will be either standing still or on the move.

If he is standing still when he receives the ball he can dribble the ball, pass it or shoot. If he chooses either of the latter two options then he cannot move with the ball. However, he can pivot. This means one foot must remain in position on the ground while the other is moved, which results in the body pivoting.

If the ball is collected while the player is on the move, he cannot progress more than two steps without bouncing or dribbling the ball.

It is important to come to a legal stop when collecting the ball on the move or at the end of a dribble and so the two-count rhythm is employed.

The first count occurs: as a player receives the ball, if either foot is touching the floor at the same time that he receives it; or as either foot touches the floor, or as both feet touch the floor, if both feet are off the floor when he receives it.

The second count occurs when, after the first count, either foot touches the floor or both feet touch the floor simultaneously. However, if a player comes to a stop after the first count, he is not entitled to the second count.

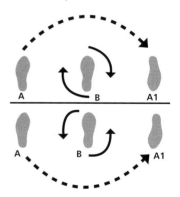

PIVOTTING
Top: *When making a forward pivot, left foot A moves to position A1 and right foot B stays in position but pivots through 180˚*
Above: *The same happens in the reverse pivot except the right foot pivots in the opposite direction*

THE TWO-COUNT RHYTHM
Once a foot has touched the floor that is 'Count 1'. The second count is when the other foot touches the floor. You must then stop. If you pivot it will be on the right foot (the back one)

When a player comes to a legal stop he may then pivot, but using the back foot only as a pivot. If neither foot is ahead of the other, he can use either foot as the pivot.

Basketball is theoretically a no-contact sport. But contact between players, either deliberately or accidentally, does occur and the rules make provisions for such incidents.

A personal foul is called against a player who makes contact with an opponent at any time whether the ball is alive or dead. A personal foul constitutes blocking, tripping, pushing, charging or holding up the progress of an opponent by extending an arm, shoulder, hip or knee, or by bending the body into any other than normal position. Rough tactics should certainly never be used.

A foul will be called if contact with the hands is made with an opponent. However, if contact is only with the opponent's hand, which is touching the ball, then no foul will be called provided the contact was made while attempting to get the ball.

If a player has five fouls called against him in a game, whether they be personal or technical fouls, he must leave the game. After seven player fouls (either personal or technical) have been called against a team in one half (NBA: four fouls per quarter), the player fouled has the right to two free throws, but he must score the first attempt in order to get a second.

The free throw

A free throw is called against a team who commits a foul. The free throw is taken from a point behind the free-throw line and in the case of a personal foul being called then the player fouled must take the throw. If a technical foul is called then any member of the non-offending team may take the free throw.

Basketball rules are basically simple but their interpretation, like those of many sports, can be complex. If you look through the rule book, you will appreciate what difficult jobs the referee and umpire have. So accept their decisions as final and please don't argue with them. Believe me, they really have a thankless task.

To go through the rules in detailed fashion would be unfair to you at this early stage of your basketball development. Therefore the Rules Clinic on the following pages has been designed to help you understand some of the finer points more clearly.

Shaquille O'Neal of the Los Angeles Lakers delights the crowds with his dazzling display of speed, power and agility

Rules
clinic

The basic rules of basketball are relatively straightforward to understand. Let's now take a look at some of the situations and questions within the rules that arise most frequently during the progress of a game.

Can a substitute come on to the court at any time?
A substitute must report to the scorer first and wait for a dead-ball situation. Following a violation, only the team who is to inbound the ball is allowed to make a substitution. However, if they do decide to bring a substitute on, then the opposing team are also entitled to do so. It may sound a bit confusing but what it means is that following a violation, the 'guilty' team cannot make a substitution UNLESS the innocent team does.

What is the difference between a violation and a foul?
Both are infringements of the rules but a violation, unlike the foul, is a breach of the rules not involving personal contact. The penalty for a violation is loss of the ball to the opposing team who take a side-line possession from the side-line nearest to where the violation took place.

If a basket is scored either during or immediately after a violation has been committed, does the goal stand?
No.

Is there any time limit for a substitute to enter the game?
No – but he must do so as quickly as possible in order to keep the game flowing. If, in the opinion of the official, there is an undue delay then a time-out will be charged against the offending team.

Can a player involved in a jump-ball be substituted?
No unless he is injured or has a blood injury that requires him to leave immediately for the dressing room and not return until the flow of blood has been staunched.

When does the thirty-seconds/twenty-four-seconds clock start?
The moment a team takes possession.

If a player takes a three-point throw at the basket and is clearly outside the three-point area at the time of the throw but his momentum, either on the ground or through the air, carries him inside the three-point area, is the basket worth two or three points if successful?
Three. The location of the player is deemed by where his feet are touching the floor. So even if he leaps through the air to make the throw, he was deemed to be outside the area at the time of the throw because that is where his feet were last positioned on the floor.

If the ball goes out-of-bounds during a team's possession and they have the right to take the side-line possession, does a new thirty-seconds/twenty-four-seconds period start?
No.

At what point is a player said to be 'in control of the ball'?
When he is holding or dribbling a live ball, or when the ball is at his disposal in an out-of-bounds situation.

What happens at the jump-ball if the ball hits the floor before either player touches the ball?
It is re-taken.

At the jump-ball can players stand where they want around the centre circle?
Yes, but no two players of the same team may occupy adjacent positions if a member of the opposing team wants one of the positions.

What happens if a non-jumper enters the centre circle during the jump-ball?
It is a violation and is penalized accordingly.

Can a player leave the court in order to gain some sort of advantage?
No. A technical foul will be called against the player and two free throws awarded.

Can a goal be scored by the ball entering the basket from underneath?
No. The ball must enter the basket from above it.

OK, so what happens if the ball DOES go through the basket from underneath?
The ball becomes dead and play is re-started with a jump-ball from the nearest circle. However, if it was deliberately thrown through the basket then it is a violation and the opposing team is entitled to a side-line possession from the side-line nearest to where the incident took place.

Can a defensive player prevent a shot from entering the basket?
Yes and no. He can attempt to stop a shot provided the ball is on its upward flight. However, if it is on its downward flight he cannot interfere with it. The restriction comes to an end once the ball hits the ring, or it is apparent it is going to miss the ring. In case of such a violation the basket will be deemed to have been made and the appropriate points awarded and play re-started from behind the end-line.

Can a player interfere with the ring or backboard to hinder a shot?
Where do you think these up from? Of course not . . . it's not very sportsmanlike is it?

If I'm in possession of the ball and an opponent touches the ball, does the clock re-start for the thirty-seconds/twenty-four-seconds rule purpose?
No.

How long does a player have to throw the ball in after a successful free throw or after it has gone out-of-bounds?
Five seconds (NBA: ten seconds). Any player taking a free throw must also do so within five seconds of the ball being placed at his disposal.

What happens if, because of so many player fouls, one team is down to only two men?
No problem, play continues with five men playing two. However, if a team is down to only one man the game is stopped and that team loses by forfeit.

If a game is lost by forfeit how is the score recorded?
If the non-offending team is in the lead at the time, then the score stands. If, by some remarkable result, they happened to be trailing, then a score of 2–0 in their favour is recorded.

Can a player shoot and score from anywhere on the court?
Yes. Don't forget shots from outside the three-point area are worth three points if successful.

Can you go over the difference between personal and technical fouls again?
Certainly . . . contact with an opponent, even if it is during a dead-ball situation or when time is dead, is a personal foul. Fouls that do not involve contact with another player are technical fouls: i.e. preventing a side-line possession being taken promptly or unsportsmanlike behaviour.

Can a technical foul therefore be called at a time other than when play is taking place?
Yes. It can be called during the interval or even before the game is started. The penalty is two free throws, after which the game will be re-started in the normal way, i.e. with a jump-ball.

What is a disqualifying foul?
A foul so bad that the official deems it necessary to dismiss the player from the court forthwith.

If a game goes into overtime, how are ends decided?
Teams continue to play to the same ends they attacked at the end of regulation time. This does not change with each subsequent period of overtime.

If a foul is committed at the same time as the timekeeper indicates the end of the half or the match, does play continue?
If free throws are part of the punishment, then time must be permitted for them to be taken.

If a player shoots for the basket and time is called before the ball enters it, do the points count?
Yes, provided the ball was in flight when time was called. Even if the ball hits the ring, rebounds, and enters the basket, the score still counts.

Does this also apply if the thirty-seconds/twenty-four-seconds time-limit expires during a throw?
Yes (FIBA). In the NBA the twenty-four-second clock is re-set only when the ball hits the rim or passes through the basket – not when it leaves the hand.

You said a coach can call two time-outs in each half. If he calls only one in the first half can he call three in the second?
No.

When is the ball out-of-bounds?
When it touches a player who is out-of-bounds, or any other person, the floor or any object on or outside a boundary line, or the supports or back of the backboards. A player is said to be out-of-bounds when he touches the floor on or outside the boundary lines.

Who takes the side-line possession if the ball goes out-of-bounds?
Normally a side-line possession is taken by a member of the team who did NOT last touch the ball.

Excellent shooting is one of the skills that all basketball players need to hone to a fine art

When dribbling, is there any restriction on the number of steps a player may take when he is not in contact with the ball?
No, he may take as many steps as he wants between bounces of a dribble . . . but he won't want to take too many otherwise he would lose possession of the ball.

Who takes the side-line possession if two players touch the ball simultaneously before it goes out-of-bounds?
No one. The referee re-starts play with a jump-ball in the nearest restraining circle.

Is play re-started with a jump-ball if the ball lodges on the ring of the basket?
Yes, from the nearest circle.

What is the penalty if a player commits a foul while his team is in possession of the ball?
A foul will be called against him, and the opposing team will take possession by taking inbounds possession from the side-line nearest to where the foul was committed.

Can a dribbler deliberately run into an opponent in order to get a personal foul against him?
Of course he can't. The dribbler should take what action he can to get past his opponent(s). Until he gets his head and shoulders past the opponent(s) the responsibility to get out of the way rests with the dribbler.

What exactly are the penalties for fouls?
Normal personal foul: The non-offending team has a side-line pos-session from out-of-bounds at the side-line nearest where the foul was committed. This does not apply when the one-plus-one rule is in force (see The Game – A Guide).
Foul on player in act of shooting: If the goal is made then it stands. In addition one free throw is allowed. If the goal is missed then two or three free throws are allowed depending on whether it was orig-inally a two- or three-point attempt at goal.
Intentional and disqualifying fouls: Two free throws are allowed. However, if the foul was against a player in the act of shooting then

the penalty is as above. After the free throws (whether successful or not), play is re-started by the team entitled to the free throws taking a side-line possession at the mid-court side-line.

If, after a personal foul, a player other than the fouled player takes the free throw does the successful basket count?
No. The correct free thrower is required to take the free throws.

If two players of opposing sides commit fouls against each other at the same time what happens?
It is called a double foul and the two players involved engage in a jump-ball at the nearest circle.

What about technical fouls, what are the penalties for them?
As with the personal foul, the offending player will have a foul charged against him and two free throws are awarded to the opposing team. Unlike the personal foul, the free throws can be taken by any player designated by the captain.

Why do players turn to the scorer's table after they have committed a foul and raise their hand?
Because the referee can require them to do this to enable the scorer to identify the guilty party so he can register all fouls against him. Remember, five fouls against a player and he is out of the game.

I know that free throws following a personal foul must be taken by the player fouled, but what happens if he is injured and cannot take the throws?
They must be attempted by his substitute.

Can players not on the court be charged with technical fouls?
Yes. Even the coach and assistant coach can have technical fouls charged against them. Anybody on the team bench so charged will also see two free throws awarded against his team, and possession is awarded out-of-bounds at mid-court to the opponents whether they are successful shots or not.

If a team is awarded free throws do they have to take them?
Yes.

POSITIONS AT A FREE THROW
This is where players must stand around the key at a free throw

■ = shooting team
● = opponents

Basket

Free-throw line

When taking free throws who stands where?
Nobody, not even one of the officials, stands inside the free-throw line. The markers along the edge of the free-throw area indicate where players may stand and the diagram shows clearly who is allowed to occupy each position. Players do not have to occupy those positions, but players of the opposing team must not occupy a position designated for the opposing side.

Right that's about it. We have clearly gone through all aspects of the game, down to some of the finer points of the rules. Now it is time to learn what to do when you get out there on the court.

NBA all-star Shawn Kemp showing off his phenomenal rebounding ability

Technique

The first thing you should realize when playing basketball is that if you haven't got the ball you can't score.

I know that is the case with many sports, but it is never more obvious than in basketball. Possession is very important. So how do you get the ball? Apart from free throws after fouls, most possession is gained: by a side-line possession from the side-line following a violation; from a side-line possession after your opponents have scored a basket; or by picking up a loose ball from a wild pass or a rebound. In the first two instances, your team is handed possession and it is down to you and your team-mates to make sure that possession is retained until an attempt at the basket is made. You can, of course, also take possession of the ball from an opponent while he is dribbling, or you can intercept a pass.

No matter how you get the ball, remember that basketball is a team passing game. Once you have possession, the ball has to be worked quickly up the court until it reaches one of your players in a good position to score a basket. Often, good attacking moves are spoilt by the shot at the basket being hurried, or taken by a player who was not in as good a position to make the shot as another. So, vision is important. Make sure you know where your team-mates are all the time. Believe me, you don't have a great deal of time to plan your next move when you get possession of the ball. That, happily, is one of the reasons why basketball is a success, because it keeps the game fast-moving and fluent.

The team

Basketball is popular because everyone can do everything – there are no positional restrictions. Each member of the team can score and each must defend. However, players are divided into three key types: guards, forwards and centres. Let's have a look at their roles.

The guards Generally the quicker players of a team, they tend to play farthest away from the opposing basket and are the men who initiate attacking moves. Like all players in a team, including the substitutes, the guards will be good handlers of the ball. But they must be specialists at long-distance shots or 'driving' to the basket and should be able to pass accurately.

The forwards They normally take up position at the side of the key and should be good shooters from the edge of the key, good passers, normally to the centre, and good rebound players.

The centres Usually the tallest players in the team they are also known as the post, or pivot, players because they take up a position close to the basket, but must be careful not to stay in the restricted area for more than three seconds. Irrespective of their height, they must be good jumpers. Naturally, they must be good close-range shooters and rebounders because they are involved in a lot of action around the basket. They should also be good passers.

The number of guards, forwards and centres depends upon the state of the match and strength and weakness of the opposition. Most teams will adopt either a 1–2–2 (1 guard, 2 forwards, 2 centres) or 2–1–2 (2 guards, 1 centre, 2 forwards) formation.

Right, that's the players and their roles. But remember that you play both an attacking and defending role while on the court. When your team has possession you are on the attack. Otherwise you have to be a defender, and thus attempt to get possession of the ball, or prevent your opponents scoring. Defence is just as an

LINE-UPS
Right: *2–1–2 attacking formation*
Far right: *1–2–2 attacking formation*

C = Centre
F = Forward
G = Guard

Before passing, hold the ball close to your body and spread your fingers around the ball

exciting part of basketball as attack but we will first look at techniques for successful attacking.

The basic skills that all basketball players should master are:

a. Passing.
b. Catching.
c. Dribbling.
d. Shooting.
e. Rebound play.

Let us look at each of these skills individually.

PASSING

The golden rule with passing is safety – don't give the ball away. Make sure the ball goes to a player in a more advantageous position than yourself and don't keep the ball in the air too long thus enabling an opponent to intercept it.

The long pass the length of the court (often called the Javelin or Baseball pass) is impressive if it is successful, but the majority of passes should be short-range to a team-mate who, like yourself, is progressing up the court. If you can keep passes down to 3–4.5m (10–15ft) or so, there is less chance of you losing possession. However, don't think that the long pass is outlawed, it certainly isn't and there are times when it should be used. For example, if a team-mate is standing unguarded near the basket then, by all means, attempt the long pass. But don't get too ambitious to begin with. Make sure you have the feel for conventional short passes before you embark on such adventurous stuff.

The pass should be made with two hands and the ball should be protected before its release, thus giving the opposition less chance of getting it.

Two things to remember about passing are: it is the safest way of keeping possession; and it is a quicker way of getting the ball down the court than dribbling. So, if you are given the alternatives, pass or dribble, you know which one to choose . . . the pass. Basketball is a team passing game.

Some important do's and don'ts of passing:
a. Make sure the pass is accurate.
b. Make the pass direct. This prevents an opponent intercepting or stealing the ball.
c. Don't pass the ball high in the air. Again, the higher the ball is in the air the longer it is out of your team's possession and thus there is more chance of the steal.
d. Make sure the pass is well-timed, particularly if the man you are passing to is on the move.

Although there are no restrictions on how the ball is passed (as long as it gets there!), there are three 'named' types of pass: the chest pass, the overhead pass and the bounce pass.

The chest pass

This is made with the ball thrown from a chest-high position. It is used more often than any other pass and is employed when there is no defender between you and the player you are passing to.

The ball is held with both hands, and by the fingers and not the palm of the hand. As the pass is executed the whole body moves forward into the pass.

Make the pass to the receiver's 'target area'. In this case, it is his outstretched right hand

A   B   C

THE CHEST PASS
The start position (A). When executing the pass, move 'into' the throw and don't stand still (B). The follow-through (C). Note how the fingers are pointing in the direction of the throw

The receiver should indicate where he wants the pass sending to by extending his hand. It will invariably be the hand farthest away from the defender, and it is to that arm that the pass should be directed.

The overhead pass

This is similar to the chest pass but is used to throw the ball over an opponent standing between you and your intended team-mate. It is held with both hands like the chest pass and the target area should again be your team-mate's signalled hand. Keep the ball in front of your head, unlike a soccer side-line possession, and use your wrists and forearms for power.

The bounce pass

This is another way of passing with an opponent in the way. This time, instead of passing the ball over him, it is passed 'under' him. The ball is 'passed' to the floor, and a single bounce takes it into your team-mate's hands. The pass should be made from the side of the body (level with the hip) as opposed to starting from a chest position, and is normally made with one hand, as opposed to two. There is a danger that this pass will be intercepted unless it is passed with speed and to a player not too far away from you.

THE OVERHEAD PASS
The start position (A). Hold the ball directly above your head and fix your eyes on the target (B). Step forward into the throw as it is made but keep the ball in front of your head, unlike the soccer throw (C). Snap your wrists to make the throw (D)

The key points to remember about passing are:

a. Know where the man is you intend passing to.

b. Keep your eyes on the target you are aiming at.

A

B

THE BOUNCE PASS
Again, look at the target area – the outstretched hand of the receiver (A). With the ball at your side, by the hip, bounce it past your opponent to your team-mate (B)

c. Aim at your team-mate's hand farthest away from his defender.

d. Follow-through with your arms after executing the pass.

Once you have made the pass don't think that's the end of your role. It most certainly isn't. You should always be moving around the court and ready to take either the return pass or another pass later in the play.

A dual at the basket between Houston's Hakeem Olajuwon and Greg Ostertag of Utah

CATCHING

There is nothing more infuriating than losing possession because a team-mate has not been able to hold a good pass. So take note of the following points and you will ALWAYS be able to catch a ball without giving it away.

The first thing to remember at all times is keep your eye on the ball. This cannot be emphasized too strongly. If you are always watching the ball it will reduce the risk of error.

You must always give the passer a target to aim at and you should indicate with your hand where you want the ball passing to. Once the pass has been made to you, take the ball with two hands and with your fingers well spread around the ball. Keep your eyes on the ball until it is safely in your possession. Once you have got the ball don't stand there nursing it. Get it safely under control ready for a pass, shot or dribble. The quicker you can control the ball the quicker you can effect your next move. Don't forget, basketball is a fast game. Don't rush, but if you slow it down too much then you may throw away any advantage your team has.

When catching the ball don't bounce it once and re-catch it because this prevents you from then dribbling; you are deemed to have dribbled by doing that. So don't get into that bad habit from the start. Once you have caught the ball, quickly decide what you are going to do: pass again, shoot or dribble.

DRIBBLING
Dribbling is done with the fingers and pads of the hand, not the palm. Don't 'slap' the ball . . .

DRIBBLING

Passing is the most effective way of moving the ball around the court. Now for another way – dribbling.

A good dribbler is a hard man to dispossess and, as we said earlier, if you don't have possession of the ball you can't score any points. So being able to dribble is a skill that every player should develop.

Dribbling is made with the fingers and pad of the hand, not the palm. The ball should not be 'slapped' but pushed down firmly, with the wrist playing a big part of the action.

As a novice you should practise dribbling by initially standing still, and then gradually moving around. Don't bounce the ball too far in front of you because, if you were in a match, your opponent would have an easy job dispossessing you.

After you have practised for a while you should have got the feel of the ball and the bounce. The next stage is to practise bouncing without looking at the ball. Top players dribble the ball at the same time as looking to see where their team-mates and opponents are at all times.

Make sure only one hand comes into contact with the ball. If both touch the ball then the dribble is deemed to be over. You have been warned.

Keep the ball between knee and waist height while dribbling and vary your dribbling between hands. It is no good being able to dribble with the right hand only. Your opponents will soon exploit this weakness. You must be able to vary your pace when dribbling so you can take an opponent unaware and go past him at speed.

Remember, basketball is a team-game, and while dribbling keeps you in possession of the ball it is doing the team no good if there is someone better placed to score. So keep your eyes on the game, not the ball, and as soon as you see a team-mate in an ideal or better position than you pass to him immediately.

. . . If you dribble with the ball too far in front of you, you are inviting a 'steal' from the opposition

SHOOTING

It is not right to say shooting is the most important element of basketball, because all skills are equally important. But let's be honest, if you cannot shoot then you aren't going to get any points and, after all, that's what the game is about.

Any player can shoot from anywhere on the court where there are no restrictions. But common sense will tell you that the closer you are to the basket the more chance there is of success. However, there will be occasions when your team is trailing, and long-distance shots (from outside the three-point circle) should be attempted in order to reduce the deficit in points.

There are five basic types of shot: the lay-up shot, the set shot, the jump shot, the free-throw shot and the close-up shot.

The lay-up shot

Used when an attacker gets the ball and, seeing no defender between him and the basket, dribbles in to the basket and jumps to shoot the ball off the backboard and into the basket. The lay-up shot will invariably be made from the right- or left-hand side of the basket. If it is made to the right, the shot is made with the right hand, and take-off is from the left foot. The sequence is, of course, the other way round if the shot is to the left side of the basket.

Don't forget though, after getting hold of the ball with both hands while dribbling, you are entitled to only two more steps so, step two should be your take-off step.

When releasing the ball, take advantage of the backboard. You don't have to throw the ball directly into the basket. If you play it gently to the square on the backboard above the ring, the ball will drop into the basket. If you hit the square too hard then the ball will most likely rebound away from the basket.

THE LAY-UP SHOT
The lay-up shot is one of the most frequently used ways of scoring

The set shot

The set shot is used when, unlike the lay-up, there is an opponent between you and the basket, but he or she is far enough away not to impede you.

With the set shot, stance is important. Your feet should point in the direction of the shot and your shoulders should be facing squarely to the basket. While the ball is held with both hands the shot is actually made with only one hand – the shooting hand. The ball rests on the finger pads of that hand. The non-shooting hand supports the ball at the side.

THE SET SHOT
Front view of the correct initial stance
(A). Side view of bringing the ball up
in front of your face (B). Straighten
your legs as the ball is delivered (C).
Concentrate on the target (D). Follow-
through and flick your wrist (E)

A   B

The ball should be released from slightly above the head.
Your eyes should be fixed firmly on the target, which can be the
ring itself or the target on the backboard. Either way, build up a
mental picture of the shot.

Your legs should be slightly bent when adopting your stance
and straightened as the throw is made. This gives you more power.
Don't forget the snap of the wrist as you make the throw. This helps
to impart backspin on the ball. And don't forget the follow-through
and the flick with your wrist.

The jump shot

The jump shot is played in the same way as the set shot except the
ball is delivered while jumping. It is used when a defender is in the
way and you make space by jumping, thus giving the defender less
opportunity to block the shot.

The jump is made vertically and the ball is delivered at the top

C   D   E

of the jump just like the set shot. However, the inexperienced player will find this shot is a difficult one to master initially. So don't attempt it until you've learned to master the set shot.

The free-throw shot

This is more or less the same as the set shot. It is awarded after a foul and every player in a team will at some stage during a match have to make a free throw. It is therefore important that you are a good free thrower.

It is like a penalty kick in soccer and the battle is between you and the basket. No other player can get in your way to prevent you scoring.

You must stand with your feet behind the free-throw line. The technique thereafter is the same as the set throw.

The beauty of the free throw is that you can practise it as much as you like and when you come to a match situation you will

THE JUMP SHOT

Preparation: fix your eyes on the target and keep your knees slightly bent (A). Bend your knees more, bring the ball to head height and jump off the ground (B) . . .

A

B

C

D

. . . Deliver the shot at the top of the jump (C). Make sure the jump is straight up – don't jump forward. Follow-through and flick your wrists (D)

THE FREE THROW

Keep your eyes on the basket and knees bent (A). Start to straighten your legs and shooting arm (B). Flick your wrist and follow-through (C). The ball is on its way to another successful basket . . . we hope

A

B

C

be faced with an identical throw. There is, of course, a matter of nerves to overcome in a match which, funnily, don't appear when you are practising on your own. Nevertheless, you must practise the free-throw shot. There is no excuse for missing it.

The close-up shot

There are occasions when you will be close to the basket and none of the previously mentioned throws can be practically carried out. This is when improvization comes in and one of the most effective close-up shots is the dunk. Simply it is a shot by a player who jumps high and throws (dunks or stuffs) the ball down into the basket. However this is an extremely difficult shot because the basket is 3m (10ft) off the ground.

Another close-up shot is the hook, which is a 'mini' version of the lay-up. It will quite often be carried out by a shooter getting

THE DUNK
The player jumps into the air and throws the ball down through the basket

THE HOOK SHOT
Getting ready for the hook. Note the position of the fingers and, of course, how the eyes are fixed on the target (A). Keep the throwing arm out-stretched, even after the ball has gone (B). The fingers impart a great deal of backspin on the ball

A   B

the ball while he has his back to the basket. He then pivots, steps and jumps to make the shot. Unlike the dunk it is not a powerful shot but a gentle one and the wrist imparts a lot of backspin as the ball hits the ring or backboard.

REBOUND PLAY

A great percentage of shots are rebounded off the backboard or the ring. This is where players under the basket must be aware of what is happening because the ball is going begging and there is a 50:50 chance of your team getting possession.

Being alert, and able to anticipate the shot and rebound are the key to good rebounding play. Good team-work and knowledge of your team-mates' skills are also a help. For example, you need to know which players are regular three-point shooters, because shots

No touching! Greg Dreiling of Dallas harasses shooter Shaquille O'Neal of the Lakers without making physical contact

taken from a greater distance tend to rebound furthest from the backboard or ring.

The centre and the forwards are generally the players assigned to rebounding duties and they should, when they anticipate a shot from a colleague, get into position in the key in readiness for a rebound. They must, bearing in mind a defender will also be in there trying to do the same thing, get into the most advantageous position before their opponent.

The rebound shot is totally unpredictable and again improvization is necessary. If possible, the ball should be collected with both hands from the rebound, and a shot made on the jump. But often it will be a case of jumping and quickly tipping the ball into the net.

So that's it from the attacker's point of view. It all sounded easy didn't it? Now we'll make the game a bit harder because we are going to introduce the defenders and look at their role and how they try to prevent the attackers from passing, catching, dribbling, shooting and winning rebounds.

THE REBOUND
Knowing there is a shot being taken, the defensive player should get between his opponent and the basket to be in a better position to get the rebound

Scottie Pippen of Chicago demonstrating excellent ball-handling skills

DEFENSIVE PLAY

The best defence is one which makes life as tough as possible for the attacking side. Harass your opponent as much as you can, without making contact with him and be prepared to help when a team-mate is beaten. There is no point in just stopping your man from scoring – it's a team game!

When standing in front of an attacker it is not only the body that should be used as a form of defence but effective use must also be made of the arms, without making contact with your opponent of course. If the attacker attempts a shot you should have your arms in the air to challenge him. The palms of the hands should be facing the ball and ready to take possession of it if the chance arises.

You should always have your knees bent ready to make a move or jump if necessary and know where the ball and the player you are marking are.

DEFENDING AGAINST THE SHOOTER
Timing is the all-important thing to remember when defending a shot

ALERT DEFENCE
Don't be taken in – you could get sold a dummy! Your opponent prepares to shoot (A) . . . you jump to defend and what happens next? He changes his mind (B)

A

B

Anticipation is the key to successful defence. That way you will prevent an attacker making a drive for the net because once he is past you there is nothing you can do about it.

You must always make it difficult for your opponent to pass and shoot. Likewise you should be alert and try to outwit your opponent at any rebound.

A good defender is one who knows the strengths and weaknesses of his opponents. If the man you are marking is, for example, only good at dribbling with his right hand, then you defend that side of him thus restricting his movement with the ball.

Because basketball is a no-contact sport the onus, more often than not, is on the defender to make sure contact is not made. You must be aware of this at all times, and be very careful. But a good defender will not need to make contact. He will be able to read the game well enough to make life tough for the attacking team.

Remember, defending is not just about gaining possession or forcing an error. It is about forcing the opponents out of their time limit as well. They have ten seconds to get the ball out of their own half, and thirty (NBA twenty-four) seconds in which to take a shot. Good defending can force them to forfeit the ball on either of those grounds. Quite often you will see an entire team employ a full court press, which is a defensive tactic designed at keeping the opponents in their own half for the requisite ten seconds. It is very effective when it comes off.

Important defensive points to remember are:

a. Always position yourself between the man and the basket, but deny him the ball.

b. Always make sure you get back to your basket before the attacking team does.

That's about it, except a final mention about practice. The beauty of basketball is that three of the game's fundamentals – passing, dribbling and shooting – can be practised on your own. (Use a wall to throw different passes against.)

In all sports it is essential to practise, and practise regularly. More importantly you should enjoy practising, but I'm sure you will enjoy basketball practice, whether it is on your own or with your team-mates.

Basketball is a great game to play and watch. We hope that

DEFENDING AGAINST THE BALL-
HANDLER
Keep your arms up in the air if your
opponent is attempting a pass (A) . . .

A

B

. . . or, if dribbling (B), keep one hand
below by the ball without contacting
the player (C)

C

Always make life tough for the player receiving a pass

through *Play the Game: Basketball* you have become more aware of the finer points of the sport no matter whether you are a player or spectator. If you are a player then we have done our bit, and the rest is up to you . . . go out and play the game, and enjoy it.

A good defensive player knows that there are times when it is sensible to avoid physical contact and so will quickly move out of the way

Useful
addresses

Australian Basketball Federation
Level 1
19–23 Hollywood Avenue
Bondi Junction
NSW 2002
Australia

Basketball Association of Wales
Connies House
Rhymney River Bridge Road
Cardiff CF3 7YZ

Basketball Canada
1600 Promenade James Naismith Drive
Gloucester
Ontario K1B 5N4
Canada

Basketball League Limited
The Lodge
Castle Bromwich Hall
Chester Road
Castle Bromwich
Birmingham B36 9DE

Basketball South Africa
PO Box 57025
Springfield 2137
South Africa

English Basketball Association
48 Bradford Road
Stanningley
Leeds LS28 6DF

**International Basketball
Federation (FIBA)**
Boschetsrieder Strasse 67
D–81379 Munich, Germany

Irish Basketball Association
National Basketball Arena
Tymon Park
Dublin 24
Republic of Ireland

National Basketball Association (NBA)
Olympic Tower
645 5th Avenue
New York, NY 10022
U.S.A.

**National Association of
Intercollegiate Athletics**
6120 South Yale Avenue
Suite 1450
Tulsa
Oklahoma 74136–4223
U.S.A.

**National Collegiate Athletic
Association**
6201 College Boulevard
Overland Park
Kansas 66211
U.S.A.

Scottish Basketball Association
Caledonia House
South Gyle
Edinburgh EH12 9DQ

USA Basketball
5465 Mark Dabling Boulevard
Colorado Springs
Colorado 80918–3842
U.S.A.

Rules clinic

index

Page numbers *in italics* indicate illustrations

B
ball
   entering basket from underneath 44
   going out-of-bounds 43, 47
   lodging in ring 48
basket
   ball entering from underneath 44
   ball lodging in ring 48
   players interfering with 44
   players preventing ball from entering 44
   time called before ball enters basket 47

D
disqualifying fouls 47, 48–9
double fouls 49
dribbling
   restriction on number of steps 48
   running into an opponent 48

F
forfeiting the game 45
fouls
   committed at end of match or half 47
   committed while own team in possession 48
   difference between personal and technical 45
   disqualifying fouls 47, 48–9
   double fouls 49
   penalties 48–9
   reducing a team to one man 45
   registering the player 49
   and violations 42
free throws
   being compulsory 49
   position of players *50*, 50
   taken by incorrect player 49
   time allowances 45
   when correct player is injured 49

I
injuries 43, 49

J
jump-ball
   ball hitting ground first 43
   non-jumpers entering the circle 44
   position of players 44
   substituting a player 43

O
out-of-bounds 43, 47
overtime 47

P
penalties for fouls 48–9
personal fouls 45
   penalties 48
   see also fouls
players
   interfering with ring or basket 44
   leaving the court 44
   position when scoring 45
   preventing ball from entering basket 44
   when in control of the ball 43

S
scoring
   ball entering basket from underneath 44
   determining location of players 43
   during or after a violation 43
   forfeiting the game 45
   position of players 45
   time called before ball enters basket 47
side-line possession 47, 48
substitutes
   coming on to court 42, 43
   and jump-ball situations 43

T
technical fouls
   penalties 49
   and personal fouls 45
   against players not on court 49
   when play is not in progress 45
   see also fouls
thirty-seconds/twenty-four-seconds rule
   ball going out-of-bounds 43
   expiring during a throw 47
   opponents touching the ball 45
   starting the clock 43
time-outs 47

V
violations
   and fouls 42
   scoring during or after 43
   and substitutions 42

index

Figures *in italics* indicate illustrations

B
back court 22
backboard 19, *20*, 21
ball *21*, 21
basket 19, *20*, 21
bounce pass 56–8, *58*

C
catching 60
centres 22, 53
charged time-outs 22–3, 36
chest pass 55–6, *56*
close-up shot *67–8*, 67–8
clothing
    officials 30
    players *22*, 21–2
contact between players 39
court 16–19, *17*, *18*

D
defensive play 53–4, *72–3*,
    72–6, *75–6*
disqualification 24
dribbling 34, *36*, 37–8, *60–1*,
    60–1
dunk 24, *67*

E
English Basketball Association
    13
equipment 16–22
extra periods 26, 36

F
fast break 25
FIBA rules
    court dimensions *17*, 19
    time periods 31
field goal 25
five-seconds rule 25, 37

forwards 25, 53
fouls *27*, 27, 28, 39, 40
free throws 12, 19, *24*, 25, 40,
    65, *66*, 67
free-throw line 18–19
front court 25
full court press 25

G
guards 25, 53

H
Harlem Globetrotters 13
held ball 25
hook shot *69*

J
javelin pass 25, *26*, 54–5
jump shot 64–5, *66*
jump-ball 12, 26, 31, *34*, 34

L
lay-up shot *62–3*, 62–3
lighting 17
line-up *54*

M
man-to-man marking 26

N
NBA rules
    court dimensions *18*, 19
    time periods 31
netball 11

O
officials 30–1
    signals *32–3*
Ollamalitzli 9
Olympic Games 11–12, 14

out-of-bounds *26*, 26
overhead pass 56, *57*
overtime 26, 36

P
passing 54–8, *55–8*
personal fouls *27*, 27, 39
pivoting *38*, 38
pok-tapok 9
possession of the ball 52–3
practice 74
professional game 13, 14

R
re-starting the game 34
rebound play 69–70, *70*
receiving the ball 38
referees 31
    signals *32–3*
restricted area 19
rules (original) 9–10

S
scoreboard 21
scorers 31
scoring 34, 36
set shot 63–4, *64–5*
shoes *22*, 22
shooting *62–9*, 62–9
socks 22
starting the game 31
    re-starting after a goal 34
strong side 27
substitutes 27

T
teams
    line-up *54*
    number of players 11
    role of players 54

technical fouls 27, 39
ten-seconds rule 27, 37
terminology 22–8
thirty-seconds /twenty-four-
    seconds operator 31
thirty-seconds /twenty-four-
    seconds rule 37
three-seconds rule 28, 37
time-outs 22–3, 28, 36
timekeeping 21, 31, 36–7
touching the ball 37
two-count rhythm 38, *39*

U
umpires 31
    signals *32–3*
unsportsmanlike fouls 28

W
weak side 28
women's game 13–14
World Championships 13–14

Y
YMCA movement 11, 12, 13

Z
zone defence 28

A Ward Lock Book • Cassell • Wellington House • 125 Strand • London WC2R 0BB

A Cassell Imprint • Copyright © Ward Lock 1998
All rights reserved. No part of this book may be reproduced or transmitted in any form or by any means,
electronic or mechanical, including photocopying, recording or any information storage and retrieval system,
without prior permission in writing from the publishers and copyright owner.

Distributed in the United States by • Sterling Publishing Co. Inc. • 387 Park Avenue South • New York NY 10016 • USA

British Library Cataloguing-in-Publication Data • A catalogue record for this book is available from the British Library

ISBN 0-7063-7717-6

Designed by Grahame Dudley Associates • Illustrations by Pond & Giles • Text revisions by Rob Dugdale

Printed and bound in Spain by Graficroma S.A., Cordoba